what I KNOW A to Z

by Fr. Dale Fushek

Copyright © 2019 Dale Fushek
All rights reserved. No part of this book may be reproduced in any form or by electronic or mechanical means, including information storage and retrieval systems, without permission in writing from the publisher, except by a reviewer who may quote brief passages in a review.

The events and conversations in this book have been set down to the best of the author's ability, although some names and details have been changed or omitted to protect the privacy of individuals.

Edited by Jody Serey

Cover art: Erika Kieny

Published in the United States by
Serey/Jones Publishers, Inc.
www.sereyjones.com

ISBN: 978-1-881276-25-8 (paperback)

DEDICATION

This book is dedicated to Rose Mofford, eighteenth governor of Arizona, and a friend without equal. Thank you, Governor Mofford. The world is a smaller planet without you.

Introduction

What I Know | Dale Fushek

The title of this book seems arrogant to me. I didn't mean it to sound that way. At this point in my life, I am well aware I know much less than I thought I knew when I was younger. I guess when we are younger, we assume having information is the same as having knowledge. When we get older, we emphasize information less and begin searching for wisdom. Wisdom has much more to do with the ability to have insight, to see the bigger picture, and to have the ability to make good judgments.

I wanted to write this book to share my heart with you. I have been through so much in my life. I have had highs that seemed to reach the stars. I have had experiences I would never have imagined I would have. I have had lows that seemed so deep I could barely lift my eyes to see the sun. My hope is that through all these highs and lows I have learned more about the meaning of life. I pray I have learned something about love. I know I have learned a lot about God. At age 66, I keep learning. I certainly keep going deeper into the mystery of God and His love. I pray within a couple of years I can write another book that can penetrate more deeply the "wideness of God's love."

I am grateful to family and friends who have walked a long journey with me. I am grateful to the Catholic church for the opportunities it has given me. Over the years, I have also learned to be grateful for the rejection by the Catholic church. It was through their rejection that I came to understand so much about God.

Introduction

I came to understand that God has not limited His truth to any denomination or person, other than Jesus. I have learned that religion and spirituality are not the same thing. In fact, religion can become a block to true spirituality. I have learned not to put my trust in human beings, but to put my trust in God. I have learned to seek the truth of God, no matter where it leads.

I would love for anyone who would like to share with me a short lesson about what they have learned in life to write to me. Perhaps with your permission, your thoughts will end up in my next book (or my next preaching.) Please write to me at:

Fr. Dale Fushek
Praise and Worship Center
2551 N. Arizona Ave.
Chandler, AZ 85225

When you title a book "A-Z" it sounds as if you are saying everything possible. After all, you have covered all the letters. But the truth is, our A-Z is just the beginning. Rather, I believe God invites us to go into a new alphabet, that is "Alpha to Omega." The book of Revelation states, "I am the Alpha and Omega, says the Lord God, the one who is and who was and who is to come, the Almighty (1:8)."

We will not have true wisdom until we pierce the meaning of God's alphabet.

What I Know | Dale Fushek

My thanks to Jody and David Serey for being my partners on this book. I am grateful to the good people who form the family of the Praise and Worship Center. You are a blessing to me. Thank you to Sandy Thiernau for her help in editing. And, thank you to my assistant Erika Kieny for the design of the book cover.

Enjoy the book. And please accept my thoughts in the Spirit they are given -- a true sense of humility, as we all stand before our Great God.

Love,
Fr. Dale

A

Addictions

What I Know | Dale Fushek

I know addictions are stronger than we think.

Addictions are hard to overcome. Sometimes, they are nearly impossible to get under control. The truth is, they never seem to be defeated, but with God's help we can learn to manage them so that they do not destroy us or those around us.

There are many different types of addictions. The problem is that some addictions are affirmed by our culture (such as workaholism and religion). Others are considered dangerous and even life threatening (such as drug and sex addictions).

Here is a list of some of the most common addictions in our culture: alcohol, smoking, gambling, video games, work, sex, exercise, shopping, prescription drugs, illegal drugs, religion, eating, and not eating. There are countless others, as well.

Medical professionals tell us that addictions are a disease of the brain that messes up our reward, motivation, and memory circuitry so that we crave immediate gratification without processing the memory of what that reward does to us. So, in a way, we give control over to a broken circuitry board in our minds. This causes our behavior to be unhealthy, inappropriate, and immature.

Addictions create problems on many levels. First, addiction is a deep spiritual problem. When you are addicted you cannot have a relationship with God. Why? Because you already have a god.

Addictions

Your god is whatever you are addicted to, and you will do anything to serve that god. If your issue is alcohol, then you will give up money, career, family, loved ones, and even your own health to serve your craving for alcohol.

Second, addictions cause relationship problems. A young person addicted to video games stops relating to their family. Workaholics spend little time with their children or spouses. Gamblers are so convinced they will win the next roll of the dice they are willing to risk the family home. They act as if they are unaware of what damage would be caused the family if the family becomes homeless.

Third, addictions cause health and wellness problems for individuals and for those around them. Smokers continue their nicotine addiction despite years of warnings. Prescription drugs and illegal drugs can destroy the heart, liver, or lungs. And, if you are in a relationship with an addicted person, the stress and worry can destroy your health and wellness as well.

So, what is at the root of addiction? For the most part, addiction seems to be the perceived need for a feeling. Perhaps it is a high, perhaps it is exhilaration, or perhaps it is the feeling of escaping. Regardless, addiction is the perceived need to feel something other than your current reality. Author Dallas Willard says, "The addict is one who, in one way or another, has given in to a feeling of one kind or another and has placed it in the position of ultimate value in his or her life."

What I Know | Dale Fushek

The only way to manage an addiction is to find someone -- or something -- that is greater than the power of the addiction. For many of us, that something is God. For others, it is nature or some higher power that is meaningful to them. That is why AA believes that the beginning of overcoming an addiction is surrendering control to a higher power.

All of us have addictions of some kind. We eat too much, work too much, or shop too much. For some, our addictions are much more critical. Hopefully for most of us, we can manage our addictions without letting them put our lives into chaos. In order to be spiritually, emotionally, and physically healthy we need to face these "demons" and surrender to our God.

Addicts need help. Local communities and churches often provide resources for those looking for the assistance and support they need. But, we can all offer patience and love. Addicted persons can rarely make progress on their own. But prayer, tough love, honest feedback, and God's amazing grace can bring help to the addict. Grace can take chaos and restore health to the life and family of an addict, and restore health to the life and family of an addict.

B
Being a Christian

What I Know | Dale Fushek

I know you cannot call yourself a Christian if you refuse to reconcile.

What does it mean to be a Christian? Does it mean you adhere to a set of theological principles? Or does it mean you live your life according to a set of moral absolutes? The answer is: to be a Christian is to surrender yourself to Christ, and, in doing so, you take His name and you live no longer for yourself, but for Him. To be a Christian means you see yourself as He sees you. It means you see others as Christ sees them. In other words, you die to yourself and you come alive (are born again) into the person of Jesus the Messiah.

St. Paul, the greatest evangelist, has an interesting take on what it means to surrender to Him. Paul believes that Christ's primary purpose was to reconcile us to God. Jesus died for our sins and through Him we have been forgiven. But reconciliation is beyond forgiveness. To reconcile means to set straight or to restore. He describes this in Second Corinthians. Paul doesn't stop there. He goes on to say that God gives us the ministry of reconciliation. "So if anyone is in Christ, there is a new creation; everything old has passed away; see, everything has become new! All this is from God, who reconciled us to Himself through Christ, and has given us the ministry of reconciliation." (II Cor. 5:17-18)

Paul continues "So we are ambassadors for Christ, since God is making His appeal through us." (II Cor. 5:20).

Being a Christian

If we surrender to Christ we seek to do His will and His work. He doesn't call us to a ministry to being "right." He doesn't call us to a ministry of being better than others or even appearing holier than others. He calls us to be His ambassador of reconciliation.

There is so much brokenness in our world. It exists in families and among friends. Church communities are over-splintered and broken. And certainly, American politics seems to be at an all-time high in terms of dysfunction and divisiveness.

We are called to do our part in healing this fractured world. And yet, there are people who say they are committed to Christ yet put no effort into healing. The question is, "How can anyone take on the name of Christ without sincerely abandoning their pride and their need to be in control and refusing to do what Christ wills for them?"

I am saddened in my own life by broken relationships. And yet people whom I have loved deeply, and who have told me they loved me, have refused to let go of the past and be made new.

If you and I want to bear the name of Christ we must bear the ministry of Christ. Words are not enough. The action of taking what was broken and making it new in Jesus is the work each of us is called to.

It is not enough to forgive. God did not stop at forgiveness with us. Rather He went past forgiveness to reconciliation.

What I Know | Dale Fushek

We can seek to do no less. And when we feel or believe we cannot reconcile ourselves, we can only seek to die to ourselves and allow God to do it through us.

I love the quote by a man named Brother Ryan. He said, "Reconciliation always brings a springtime to the soul."

I believe he is right. And, in my experience, it always brings light to a sometimes-dark world.

> The action of taking what was broken and making it new in Jesus is the work each of us is called to.

C

Change

What I Know | Dale Fushek

I know that pain can motivate change.

Dr. Henry Cloud and Dr. John Townsend wrote, "We change our behavior when the pain of staying the same becomes greater than the pain of changing."

In other words, we don't change unless it's painful not to change.

None of us likes hardship. And, none of us likes pain. In fact, we do all we can to avoid hurt. From the time we are born, we learn to avoid pain and discomfort.

As children, we obey our parents and teachers out of fear of being punished. As we age, and the consequences of our actions become more serious, we are even more motivated to stay out of trouble.

Our culture has turned comfort into a god. We value being comfortable above almost everything else. People even pick their church by what church is closest, or which church has the most comfortable seats. We like being comfortable.

We avoid physical pain, emotional pain, and spiritual pain. Many of us have learned great avoidance skills. We have learned to even avoid the truth.

Change is usually uncomfortable. To make a major life change is hard. It's uncomfortable to change jobs. It's uncomfortable to terminate a relationship. It's uncomfortable to stop drinking.

Change

We don't like change. But, as Cloud and Townsend said, when the pain of not changing gets bad we often find our motivation. Dis-ease and dis-comfort can be a blessing in our lives if they help us move ahead.

From a physical point of view, it often takes a dis-ease to make us change. When I found it getting harder to breathe, I went to the doctor and began to change my diet so I could lose weight. It took pain and dis-ease to move me.

The same is true of our emotional life. Unless someone is in emotional pain, they often will not change. This seems to be especially true in marriage.

Married couples often go many years without confronting the fact they don't communicate, and the marriage has become lonely. Sometimes people stay together for financial reasons even though the relationship has become abusive and destructive. The comfort of a familiar lifestyle can be a great motivator to stay the course.

Spiritual pain works the same way. Many people will not seek to go deeper in their relationship with God out of fear. It's not until what they were told during childhood about God stops working that they will seek new insight.

I am not trying to tell you that I like pain. I don't. I have had plenty of it in my life. I have never gotten used to it. And, I certainly don't seek it. I have also learned that it is not something to fear or avoid at all costs.

What I Know | Dale Fushek

I have learned that pain is often the doorway God uses to come into my life. It was in the darkest time of my life that I came to know God's unconditional love in a deeper way than I had ever known before.

The great spiritual writer Brennan Manning wrote, "One of life's greatest paradoxes is that it's in the crucible of pain and suffering that we become tender."

Pain often has the potential to make us more compassionate with others and with ourselves. We learn, as we abandon ourselves, that God will transform our pain, and in doing so transform our hearts. It is in the act of dying to self that we are born again into God and into new life. Facing painful truth frees us, transforms us, and changes us into better people and more committed Christians.

Suffering for the sake of suffering has no value. But suffering in order to change, is worth more than gold.

D

Devotion

What I Know | Dale Fushek

I know that loyalty and devotion seem to be ancient relics.

I am a dinosaur. I know I am. Many of my values and beliefs are old school. I believe that loyalty is a great virtue, and I also am aware that many young people have no idea what loyalty truly is.

I shop at a locally owned grocery chain. I know the owners well and I know they do a lot to help the poor of our community. I will pay a few pennies more to support them because I know the money stays in our local community.

I stayed at the same bank for over 30 years until they wouldn't help me when I needed to re-finance. Another bank did help and I will stay with them for a long time. I am loyal to my country, my teams, my college, my family, my friends, and my God. Loyalty is very important to me.

Loyalty and devotion are closely related. The word "devotion" comes from a Latin word devotus which means to be dedicated to something or someone by a vow. The word "loyalty" originally referred to allegiance to your country or your ruler. Both of these words are strong words which indicate deep feelings. These feelings motivate people to action. These actions lead people to war, make people wear special shirts to a game and jump up and down in support of a team, drive a bit further to support a friend's store, and stay with a company as an employee for more than a few months. To me personally, loyalty means to share hearts with someone or some institution. Loyalty goes beyond thoughts. It goes to the heart. And, loyalty creates a connection that is a hard bond to break.

The opposite of loyalty is disloyalty. I understand there are a lot of reasons that provoke people to be disloyal. Few companies are loyal to their employees. In fact, few companies have any kind of loyalty to their customers. Companies would rather lose a customer than take time to give the service it would take to keep a customer. I know all of this is true. And I know it is the way of the world today. But I don't have to live the way of the world. I want to live differently. I want to be loyal. I want to reward companies that are loyal. Loyalty and devotion in business are refreshing and build a solid foundation in a community.

I believe that loyalty is crucial to living with honor. I believe in building relationships. Relationships build trust between people. Relationships build a culture in which people feel safe and certain they will be treated fairly. Even in business, the word between two friends should be a bond. The comedian Jerry Lewis said, "I have a loyalty that runs in my bloodstream."

He went on to say, "Don't give me a paper or contract. I can get the same lawyer who drew it up to break it. But if you shake my hand, that's for life."

Patriotism is a form of loyalty and devotion. Faithfulness to our church community is a form of loyalty and devotion as well. Faithfulness to friends, even when things go bad, is a

What I Know | Dale Fushek

virtue in God's eyes. The book of Proverbs (18:24) states, "Friends come and friends go, but a true friend sticks by you like family."

The most important form of loyalty is our loyalty to God. The way we remain loyal to God is by keeping His commandments. As Christians, we must be loyal to Christ and His value system. The values of Christ include: love, mercy, compassion, generosity, refusal to judge others, and valuing human life. In our loyalty to Christ, we must cherish the giver of all life. We must treat the unborn, people who are different than us -- even our enemies -- with respect. If we don't build a relationship with Christ, we will never have the grace to be truly loyal to Him. Religion doesn't build loyalty. A relationship with God will build the virtue of loyalty.

I don't judge anyone who makes the decision to abandon a friend, an employer, or a country. I just know who I want to be. I want to be a loyal person. And, all I can do is invite you to do the same.

E

Evil

Evil is the opposite of grace.

Grace is God's life in us.

Evil

I know that evil thrives in chaos.

Most of us, in my generation, watched the church lady on Saturday Night Live. We laughed at her self-righteousness. We also laughed each time she said the phrase, "Could it be Satan?"

It was a funny skit. But evil is no laughing matter.

I am not a devil chaser. I don't look for little demons around each corner. I do know, however, that evil is very real. I have also come to understand that evil is very subtle. Evil works in chaos. It causes chaos. It flourishes in chaos. It succeeds in chaos. Evil causes disharmony in families, communities, churches, and our own nation. And, as long as there is chaos, it is difficult to hear the voice of God and the voice of truth.

I have also come to understand that chaos is sometimes just another word for drama. We all know people who are drama "queens" or "kings." They tend to be so self-absorbed that their own neediness shifts attention to them and to their wants. Drama people tend to put the "funk" in dysfunctional.

Whenever our world is flooded with drama, dysfunction, and self-absorption the result is always the same -- chaos, chaos, and more chaos. In the midst of all that chaos it is easy to forget who we are and who God is. It is easy to lose our sense of right and wrong. And, it is easy to be so caught up in the moment that God and His teaching is lost.

What I Know | Dale Fushek

We begin to believe we don't need God and that we can and need to be in control to make things right.

Evil is the opposite of grace. Grace is God's life in us. It is the strength and wisdom of God working in our midst. Grace can only work in truth because grace is God's presence and God's life.

If you are a drama queen or king -- knock it off. That behavior is not holy and it is not of God. If you are self-absorbed or overly needy, let go of it. You are blocking God and allowing the evil one to be in control of your life and your surroundings. And, if you live or are involved with someone who is dysfunctional, get help because they are draining grace right out of your life.

And, as far as our country goes -- if we don't end the chaos of hatred, fighting, wrestling for control, and needing to have things our way, we will destroy our nation and all it stands for. Years ago, our country was warned by an enemy leader that he did not need to destroy us. He told us he was confident we would destroy ourselves from within on our own. I pray he was not foretelling our future. It looks like, however, he was pretty accurate. Our nation and our government are in chaos.

As the church lady used to ask, "Could it be Satan?"

F

Friendship

What I Know | Dale Fushek

After many years of trusting everyone, I learned there are very few people we can truly trust.

Friendship

I know it is important to know who to trust.

There is a huge difference between being friendly and having a friend. We should be friendly with everyone. To be friendly means you are kind, caring, engaging, and make others around you feel comfortable. But, at the same time, we should be careful about choosing our close friends.

The Bible offers profound wisdom about friendship. Proverbs 18:34 says, "A man of many companions may come to ruin, but there is a friend who sticks closer than a brother."

Proverbs 17:17 tells us, "A friend loves at all times, and a brother is born for adversity."

In the New Testament, Jesus says, "Greater love has no one than this, than someone lay down his life for his friend." (John 15: 13).

In other words, the Bible sets high standards for friendship.

Other writers also have given us great insight about friendship. C.S. Lewis said, "Friendship is the greatest of worldly goods. Certainly, to me it is the chief happiness of life. If I had to give a piece of advice to a young man about a place to live, I think I would say 'sacrifice almost everything to live where you can be near your friends'."

Henri Nouwen said, "Friendship is one of the greatest gifts a human being can receive. It is a bond beyond common goals, common interests, or common histories. It is a

What I Know | Dale Fushek

bond stronger than sexual union can create, deeper than a shared fate can solidify, and even more intimate than the bonds of marriage or community. Friendship is being with the other in joy and sorrow, even when we cannot increase the joy or decrease the sorrow. It is a unity of souls that gives nobility and sincerity to love. Friendship makes all of life shine brightly."

Friendship has levels. And, over time through a variety of experiences, those levels either deepen or the friendship breaks. Sometimes in our desire to not be alone we bring a so-called "friend" into our inner circle long before we should when the relationship has not been tested with time and adversity. This is when many hurts and disappointments can occur.

After many years of trusting everyone, I learned there are very few people we can truly trust. I used to think that kind of statement sounded cynical, but now I understand that it is simply truth. Trust, which comes from an ancient word which means confidence, means that I am confident the other person will not abandon me, judge me, turn on me, ignore me, or betray me.

After going through a painful time in my life, where some in whom I had total confidence actually did betray me, I understand that I had expectations of love they did not share with me. What I heard when they said "I love you" was they were willing to lay down their lives for me. I know that is what I meant when I told them I loved them. But

Friendship

when pressure came, they walked the other way. Like first responders, a true friend is one who rushes in when everyone else is headed the other direction.

So now, I am grateful to have a few long-time friends. I am cautiously open to others and I have lowered my expectations of others. I am not cynical about friendship. I simply have a clearer understanding of the levels of friendship and I am careful about moving to a deeper level.

I subscribe to the theory of there being four levels of friendship:

(1) Acquaintance: familiar with each other, know public information about each other

(2) Casual friendship: share common interests, activities, and concerns

(3) Close friendship: share life, goals, faith

(4) Intimate friendship: invest in each other's lives, help each other mature, seek God together.

I personally have to take responsibility for those I chose to trust and who walked away from me. I made presumptions they either never made or were not capable of making. I moved casual friends or close friends into the "intimate" category and perhaps they had no intention of doing the same with me.

Friendship on any of the four levels is a good thing. It is

What I Know | Dale Fushek

good to know people and to have people with whom to share activities. Loneliness is not a good thing and none of us desires to be unable to share life with others. We should simply exert caution. And, in our minds and hearts, we should not move others to a deeper level until we know they are capable of doing so, and want to do so.

Friendships can cause pain. They can also lead to our greatest joys. It's simply a matter of doing what's right for both you, and the other person.

"A faithful friend is a sturdy shelter. He who finds one finds a treasure. A faithful friend is beyond price." (Sirach 6:6)

G

God

What I Know | Dale Fushek

When we can surrender to God, we actually taste a bit of heaven on earth.

God

I know there is a God, and it is not me.

One of my favorite movies is *Rudy*. For the sake of disclosure, I will state that I attended Notre Dame and I understand this fact colors my view of this movie. To summarize, the young man Rudy is doing everything he can to be accepted into Notre Dame. No one in his family has ever gone to college and everything is stacked against him. In one of the scenes, Rudy is sitting in the church at the university. One of the priests walks through and stops to talk to him. Rudy questions why he hasn't been admitted to the college, and the priest says, "I have learned one thing. There is a God and it is not me."

It sounds so simple to say those words. But the truth is that most of us never learn this basic lesson. We spend most of our lives trying to be in control. We learn as children to try to control our parents. As young adults we try to control those around us. And then as adults, we try to control our spouse, our children, our bosses, and when we can, we try to even control the institutions that influence us. We can end up frustrated, angry, and bitter people. It rarely ends up "pretty."

Some of you reading this will say, "Nope, not me."

Well, after more than 40 years in ministry I can tell you that if you are right, YOU are the exception. I have learned that 95 percent of us are control freaks. At least 4 percent of us are liars. That doesn't leave a whole lot of people who have truly learned to let God be in control.

What I Know | Dale Fushek

Some of us are obvious in our desire to control. We shout, throw tantrums, get violent, or bully others in order to get what we want. Some of us are more subtle: we cry, make others feel guilty, and play the martyr role. Regardless of what method we use, we seek the same thing. Control.

Our desire to be in control also comes out in our judgements toward others. In our own minds, and then sometimes even in our "outside voice" we speak our disapproval of others. We elevate our own opinions and we are sure we know what God is thinking about a certain subject or person. Our opinions and judgements are just other ways we try to force others to live by our standards and meet our expectations.

I have seen in my years of pastoral counseling so many people who had their self-esteem destroyed by other family members trying to control them. A child can be damaged by an over-controlling parent. A spouse's self-esteem can be harmed by a husband or wife not respecting the other person's judgement or opinions. In other words, important relationships can be severely damaged by a controlling person even to the point that someone can feel abused and resentful.

Out of the Ten Commandments, the most broken commandment is still the first one: "I am the Lord your God; you shall have no false Gods before me."

We can become our own false God.

God

So, how do we stop this unhealthy behavior? Do we just stop having opinions? Do we have to live with no expectations of others? Should we stop trying to make good things happen for ourselves, others, and the world? Does God want us to sit by and just be observers of life?

The truth is, it doesn't have to be either/or. We can and should work hard. We should have positive expectations for others and for ourselves. And we will always have opinions about how things should go. We should be making a difference in the world and with our loved ones. We are called to be "coaching each other upwards" so we can all be better and more successful people.

BUT -- it's what we do, think, and feel, that matters when things do not go our way on our time schedule. It's the ability to surrender to something or someone bigger than we are. It is the knowledge that we only see partially and that the only one who sees it all is God.

The word "surrender" is not a word we like to use. However, in the spiritual life, it is the essential stance we must take when we stand before God. We must be willing to surrender our opinions, judgements, wants, and even needs to a higher power. In other words, we need to let God be God. Let Him be the creator, and us accept our role as His children.

As a priest and pastor, I have sat beside many people who were near death. It is amazing that at that moment some

What I Know | Dale Fushek

folks are still wrestling with God. They want to live and won't let go, won't surrender. These folks have difficult and unpeaceful deaths. The result is the same. They ultimately (or at least their bodies do) surrender to God. The ones who are at peace and surrender their lives to God step gracefully into new life.

Every day we are called to have little deaths. These little deaths teach us that "there is a God and it is not me." And in this process, we learn that the very act of surrender, which involves dying to ourselves, always leads to a larger, more beautiful life than we ever imagined. When we can surrender to God, we actually taste a bit of heaven on earth.

God is the God of life. His desires for us are even more loving than our desires for ourselves. We state our opinions. We work hard for what we think is best. But ultimately, we surrender to God's timing -- God's will.

You may be a very smart person. You may be very wise. As a pastor, I may be seen by other people as well-educated and wise with experience. But, you know, and I know in our heart of hearts, that we are not what others see. We need God. The earlier in life we learn this simple lesson, the better off we will be. We will throw fewer tantrums, cause less destruction to those around us, and we will have peace in our hearts.

There is a God, and it is not me!

H

Humor

What I Know | Dale Fushek

I know we need to laugh more.

A dear friend of mine, humorist and author Erma Bombeck once said, "There is a thin line that separates laughter and pain, comedy and tragedy, humor and hurt."

Erma chose to spend her life (she died in 1996) making people laugh. She was good at it. And, she was right. Life is so fragile that often laughter and pain can happen at the same time.

We need more Erma Bombecks. Erma had a way of seeing things differently. She could find humor in the most mundane, ordinary things: families, dirty clothes, dinners, and relationships. Where others saw stress, she found a way to find something to laugh at.

I believe we have a God of laughter. There are different ways to make people laugh. Some people mock other people. Some use anger. And, some use sexual thoughts or foul language to try to be funny. These "senses of humor" are not healthy and they are not about God laughter. God laughter involves delighting in another person, finding joy in a difficult situation, or seeing humor in innocent human behavior.

Psychologists have developed a new form of treatment called "laughter therapy." They have discovered that laughing is a great way to reduce stress and cope with life. Laughter seems to help our bodies release stress-busting endorphins. These endorphins deaden our stress and pain

Humor

and allow us to live a more balanced life. I recently heard of a new exercise called "laughter yoga." The claim is that laughter is an exercise of the body and not just the mind, so whenever we laugh, we help ourselves strengthen muscles and heal our bodies. (I know that if I performed yoga in a crowd, somebody would be laughing – that's for sure.)

Even though the medical world tells us that laughter is an action of the body, I believe it is an action of the soul as well. The Gospel of John tells us that Jesus came so that "We might have life and have it to the fullest" (John 10:10). God desires for us to be filled with joy. He gives us a joy the world cannot give and a joy that the world cannot take away.

When I first entered ministry, I tried to bring laughter into my homilies, teachings, and church services. At the time, there were those who thought I wasn't taking what I was doing seriously and that by getting people to laugh I was minimizing the sacredness of worship and prayer. I never intended that. On the contrary, I found that laughter united the community in a unique way. I also found that laughter made God much more intimate and personal.

Laughing at another person is never holy or sacred. But, laughing at ourselves, our lives, and things that we take way too seriously gives us a new way of seeing life with a new and holy perspective. It's not only okay to laugh -- it is holy to laugh.

What I Know | Dale Fushek

The funny and famous Joe Garagiola frequently pointed out that he was tired of hearing a letter from Paul to the Corinthians. He wanted to hear their response back to Paul. This was a good observation from Joe -- and wouldn't it be good if someone wrote back to Paul on behalf of their community? It might get folks to tune in at church.

So, laugh. It's good. It's holy. It's healing. As someone said, "Sometimes I laugh so hard the tears run down my leg."

If that should ever happen, maybe you would hear a chuckle or two come right down out of heaven.

Even though the medical world tells us that laughter is an action of the body, I believe it is an action of the soul as well.

I

Integrity

What I Know | Dale Fushek

I know we need a good dose of integrity.

Many years ago, I took a lie detector test. It was stressful. I did well on it except for one question. The test administrator asked me if while I was in the seminary, had I "ever taken credit for academic work you did not do?"

I panicked. I was sure I was guilty, but I couldn't think of anything specific. I was sure I must have copied something out of an encyclopedia without referencing it properly. I was certain I must have copied someone else's thoughts out of a book and presented their insights as if they were my own ideas.

So, I answered, "yes." The test indicated I wasn't being truthful.

None of us is perfect when it comes to telling the truth. At some point in our lives we have told white lies or exaggerated the truth. Unfortunately, being less than honest has become a lifestyle for many people in our world. Lying on Facebook, defrauding stores, shoplifting, and stealing someone else's identity have all become commonplace.

Proverbs 12:22 states, "The Lord detests lying lips, but He delights in people who are trustworthy."

Wow!

Scripture makes it clear that God desires for us to walk in integrity and truth. The word integrity derives from a Latin term meaning "soundness, wholeness, and uncorrupted."

Integrity

In English by the year 1548 the word "integrity" meant "a sense of honesty and uprightness."

Today, the word generally means "the quality of having strong moral principles."

As soon as we start addressing the topic of integrity many people immediately think of politicians. And, it is true that many of our politicians seem to lie and mislead. In the old days (and now I am really sounding like an old man), the media tended to try to hold politicians to the truth. Now, media folks lie as much or more than the politicians they used to hold accountable. Unfortunately, there seems to be no one to hold media to the truth.

And, no doubt, we are all partially to blame when it comes to the politicians. Sometimes they are afraid to be honest about their past because the public won't accept the fact that people can change. Many of us are way too busy trying to blame or embarrass those we disagree with. It is all very messy, and everybody gets dirty.

To acknowledge the mess we are in when it comes to integrity, we have to look in the mirror. We need to hold ourselves to high standards of truth. We need to be honest about our pasts. We need to be honest about our mistakes. And, we need to be honest in our daily dealings with each other.

We only have control over ourselves -- no one else. That means we must be honest with money and in business.

What I Know | Dale Fushek

We need to have integrity and keep commitments we make. Our word must be our bond, and our promises must be kept.

God works only in truth. He heals in truth. His glory shines in truth. No amount of justification or rationalization can allow us to lose our integrity.

St. Paul, in his letter to the Hebrews (13:18) states, "Pray for us, so we are sure we have a clear conscience and we desire to live honorably in every way."

This is a prayer request we can all make.

Someone else once said, "One of the truest tests of integrity is its blunt refusal to be compromised."

In other words, whether we are taking a lie detector test or not, we must speak with integrity.

Oprah Winfrey observed, "Real integrity is doing the right thing knowing that nobody's going to know whether you did it or not."

No matter what the politicians or media choose to do, we need to be bathed in the truth.

Author Brene Brown wrote, "Integrity is choosing courage over comfort; choosing what is right over what is fun, fast, or easy; and choosing to practice our values rather than simply professing them."

Jesus said simply "the truth will set you free." (John 8:32).

J

Justice

What I Know | Dale Fushek

I know there is little justice in this world, and very little in the next.

Whenever someone comes into my office for spiritual counseling, and they are involved with the court system in any way, I always alert them by saying, "We don't have a justice system in America; we have a legal system."

As I say the words, I feel like I am being very negative and pessimistic. However, the person in front of me often responds "I think you are right."

The word "justice" comes from a Latin word justus which means "equitable, fair, and upright." Often, professionals involved in the legal system seem to be more concerned with their own careers, how things appear in the media, and their own political beliefs instead of being fair and righteous. A prominent lawyer once remarked, "It's not about innocence or guilt. It's about whether you can win the case or not."

Judges, attorneys, and even some law enforcement can have their own agendas and how a case is carried out often depends on elements other than justice. Punishment is often given out in unequal ways. And, some people are prosecuted simply as a public example. I have learned, and I share with others -- stay out of the legal system as much as you can.

So, what about God? Don't the scriptures tell us that God is a just God? True, the Bible does tell us that God is just.

Justice

To me that means that God is never unjust and that no one is ever treated unfairly. The Acts of the Apostles states He "shows no partiality (Acts 10:34)."

God knows what it righteous and what is fair. God, however, does not use justice as His measuring stick. God has a "mercy system." God knows what everybody has done in their lives and what each person deserves. But He does not impose punishment or embarrassment upon others based solely on justice. His mercy outweighs His justice. Mercy is a gift, a kindness which replaces what the person deserves.

I love the story about a judge in a small town who has a teenage son. The son commits a crime of speeding through the town. When the court date arrives, the boy appears before the town judge who happens to be his dad. The judge hears the case and imposes a strict fine upon the young man. When the trial has ended, the judge steps down from the bench, takes off his robe, and walks over to the bailiff with his teenager. The dad puts his arm around the son, takes out his wallet and pays the fine. This is what our God and Father has done for us. He knows our crimes (sins) and through His Son He has already paid our debt.

So, what does this mean to us? Well, first of all, if you are involved in the U.S. Court system, recognize that it is a legal system and do not be disappointed if you do not receive justice. Second, when you die, don't expect justice. Know that we have God who knows justice but chooses

What I Know | Dale Fushek

mercy. And, third, if there is going to be more justice in the world, we need to be the ones who bring it to our society. Justice is a good thing. We should do our best to treat everyone with justice. We should treat all people with equal respect and with a sense of fairness.

And, by the way, since we are believers -- it would be good for us to go beyond justice and imitate our Father by showing each other some mercy. Justice tempered with mercy is immensely powerful.

We don't have a justice system in America; we have a legal system.

K

Kick Off

What I Know | Dale Fushek

I know the NFL owns Sunday.

My greatest love is leading worship. My training, other than generic seminary training, is in liturgy and worship. I had the opportunity to study worship at the University of Notre Dame and to obtain a Master's degree in liturgy. Key to understanding Christian worship is understanding the meaning and importance of Sunday.

For the Jewish people keeping the sabbath was not only a commandment but a sign of the covenant between them and Yahweh. As Christianity unfolded as a movement, then as a religion, the meaning of the sabbath changed to Sunday.

St. Paul rejects the Jewish tradition of Saturday sabbath in favor of the new creation in Christ. In the Gospels, it is clear that the resurrection of Jesus happens on Sunday. All of the appearances of the resurrected Jesus happen on Sunday. St. Paul makes it clear that Sunday is the day for Christians to assemble. Constantine actually makes Sunday the legal holiday for the Roman Empire in 321. Eventually, all of Europe and most of the world came to celebrate Sunday as a day of rest and worship.

In our own culture, Sunday was unique and important. Local communities enacted "blue laws" in order to keep it holy. Blue laws restricted purchases of alcohol either entirely, or before noon, and did not allow bars to open until church services were over. In other words, culture gave re-

Kick Off

ligion -- especially Christianity -- a great show of support by recognizing the importance of church and Sunday services.

In recent years, there has been a major shift in understanding Sunday. It started with early kick-offs for the NFL. All of a sudden, games were on television by 10:00 on Sunday morning. Pre-game shows replaced the religious and news shows that typically were shown on Sunday mornings. Blue laws were removed and the entire culture shifted from Sunday being a church day to Sunday as football day.

I find it fascinating that stadiums have become athletic cathedrals and liturgical rituals have shifted to half-time rituals. Football has become a sort of religion to our culture and to many people.

It is not the responsibility of our government or our culture to force us to keep Sunday holy. Blue laws are not needed and the NFL has the right to play football any day at any time. But, we as Christians need to reclaim Sunday as the Lord's day. We have to be the ones to remember that Sunday is the day of Jesus' rising to new life. We have to remember that the Holy Spirit was poured upon the church on Sunday. Sunday is the day of Emmaus and communion. Sunday is the day that marks our relationship with God.

I have to be honest and tell you that I am a big NFL fan. I love watching football. I believe Church and football can

What I Know | Dale Fushek

both take place on Sunday. I also know that I need to delay kick-off until I have finished worship and I have finished gathering with the Christian community. As for me, I tend to pray a lot on Sunday afternoon and evening as I watch my favorites teams.

I don't know if that makes Sunday any holier but I do know I must always give God preference. Even the Super Bowl doesn't outrank my loyalty to God. Super Bowls come and go. Heaven will be forever.

> Football has become a sort of religion to our culture and to many people.

L

Love

What I Know | Dale Fushek

I know learning to love takes a lifetime.

When I was 17 years old, I lay in bed one night thinking about my future. For some reason, I pictured myself on my death bed. I asked myself, "What do I want to look back on and say I have accomplished?"

My answer was simple and inspired (by God): I wanted to learn how to love. I didn't have any idea what that meant or how I would do it, but I knew I would have to learn love from God.

Like you, I had heard the word "love" from the moment I was born. Family members would often say "I love you." Others talked about loving Big Macs and ice cream.

As I got older, I was told not to "make love" to the girls I knew. And probably like you, throughout those years, no one ever told me exactly what the word "love" really means. So, after all these years, what have I learned about love?

First of all, love is not a feeling. I know it involves feelings, but it is not a feeling. It is a decision. Love is a commitment.

I know that love is not conditional and it is not the opposite of hate. Love involves self-gift, it is other-centered, and it demands nothing in return. St. Paul tells us that love is patient and kind. He also tells us that love involves charity, compassion, and creating a safe place for another person.

Love

Love is ultimately the decision and action of putting someone else above one's own wants and needs.

Scripture teaches us a lot about love. In fact, the word "love" appears about 200 times in the New Testament. Jesus is the master of love, and His example is the measuring stick of authentic love. His death on the cross and His call to lay down our lives for our friends become the greatest teaching we have about love.

Many writers, poets, and psychologists have taught us about love, as well. Some of what they say is helpful. Some of it misses the target completely. For instance, many psychologists say that we can love for a season of life. This is contrary to the Bible which teaches us that love never ends. Psychologists seem to be right on target, however, when they tell us that we human beings are pre-wired in our brains for a connection with love. We seem to have been created for this.

Love is ultimately the willingness to die to self and to begin to live for others. Love is not dysfunctional or weak. Sometimes love demands a toughness and strength beyond what we can even imagine. During terrible times, we learn that we are simply instruments of God's love.

Children can love in a beautiful way. Young people can have tremendous insight into love and relationships. Maybe that's what is meant by the old saying, "It takes one a long time to become young."

What I Know | Dale Fushek

But for the most part, it seems to take many years and a lot of failures in order to really understand love.

None of us has ever been loved perfectly by another human being. And none of us has ever loved another being (human or divine) in a perfect way. But, through grace and the Holy Spirit, God continues to give us insight into what love is. God will continue to show us that He is love incarnate.

I have often said I would like to have the words, "He loved" on my tombstone.   Perhaps by the time God calls me to heaven I will "get it."

I think I am getting better at it, and I am using my years of life learning day by day how to love.

Love is ultimately the willingness to die to self and to begin to live for others.

M

Money

What I Know | Dale Fushek

I know money has purpose.

Over the years much has been said about money. Some people say, "Money cannot buy happiness."

Others say, "It sure helps."

The Bible states, "The love of money is the root of all kinds of evil."

Thomas Jefferson said, "Never spend your money before you earn it."

And, financial guru Dave Ramsey said, "We buy things we don't need with money we don't have to impress people we don't like."

He also tells us to "act your wage."

Since so many people have opinions about money, I will give you mine. I believe that money has two purposes: survival, and to show love.

Let me explain.

Clearly, the main purpose of money is to live. Money is simply a human invention used to replace the barter system. Instead of trading chickens for medical care, we sell chickens for money, and then pay our doctors with cash. The doctors then use the money to buy chicken sandwiches for their families.

It's simply a step up from the old-fashioned barter system.

Money

The truth is, money has become so important and complex that it's created banks, the stock market, and countless scams aimed at people who want more money fast and easy.

Money is essential in our world for food, housing, health care, education, utilities, transportation, and hundreds of other things needed to survive in a modern society. Parents work long hours for their families in order for them to have a safe place to live, food to nourish them, and decent clothing to keep them protected from the elements. When money is used for living with dignity, it takes on a dignity that we don't always assign to "dirty green paper."

The second purpose of money is to show love. I believe we show God our love when we tithe. Tithing also shows our trust in God. When we give donations to the church, the poor, or to medical research, we show our love of others.

We show love (our love and God's love) when we feed the hungry. We show love and compassion when we reach out to others and give to Alzheimer's or cancer research. We show love to our community when we give to our churches and support the work that they do in preaching and teaching the truth.

We show love when we buy gifts for others. We show love when we go the extra mile and help our young sons and daughters live out their dreams by going to college.

We show love when we send a card or flowers to some-

What I Know | Dale Fushek

body who is sick or grieving. When we use money in this way, we give money great dignity and purpose.

I believe when we do some things for ourselves, we demonstrate self-love. Self-love is not the same as selfishness. When we further our education, buy ourselves a safe car, or treat ourselves (within reason) to a well-earned vacation, we are loving ourselves in a healthy way.

Having said all of this, I will agree that a lot of money is used for selfishness such as reckless gambling, and potentially destructive drugs and alcohol abuse. There is the unhealthy and unloving intent of money when we use it to try to control others, buy influence, or use it to harm others.

Money, like so many other things, is neither good nor bad of and in itself. Money either takes on dignity when we use it right for living and loving, or becomes a vehicle for greed and evil when we use it for unloving purposes.

N

No Leaders

What I Know | Dale Fushek

I know we lack leaders.

I love Charles Barkley. He makes me laugh, and he actually offers great insight. Although I really do not know him as a friend, I have met him on several occasions. Barkley shocked the world when he did a Nike commercial in 1993 and said, "I am not a role model."

Charles was right. He is not a leader, nor a role model. But he is a great example of someone who worked very hard at perfecting his craft. He came out of a tough background and became highly successful. I believe in general he is a good man who represents success. However, Charles is not someone we would want to imitate in our own lives. This is not a condemnation of Barkley. I believe this is what he was telling us in the long-ago Nike commercial.

If we look at the world today, we can find a lot of good examples to follow. There are great athletes who are examples of hard work and dedication. And, there are business people who are models of entrepreneurship and creativity. There are even politicians who are good examples of service and compassion. But good examples are not the same as leaders.

It has been said that a leader is someone who knows the way, goes the way, and shows the way. Henry Kissinger said, "The task of a leader is to get his/her people from where they are to where they have not been."

No Leaders

I like what singer/actor Mark Wahlberg said: "I pray to be a good servant to God, a father, a husband, a son, a friend, a brother, an uncle, a good neighbor and a good leader to those who look up to me, a good follower to those who are serving God and doing the right thing."

The word "lead" is an old English word meaning "to show the way, guide." Leading others means inspiring others to follow. A leader can articulate a vision that others can see and believe in. A leader is not just an example of a particular virtue or good trait; leadership is a gift that goes far beyond being a role model.

Who are leaders of the past? Joan of Arc, George Washington, Abraham Lincoln, Winston Churchill, Eleanor Roosevelt, Martin Luther King, Nelson Mandela, Mother Teresa, and Billy Graham, to name a few. Of course, there are countless more. Some are unknown to the wider population but inspired people in their own sphere of influence. I am sure there are many people like that today. But, where are the leaders who can move us from disunity to unity, from dysfunction to being able to function as a society, and from hatred to compassion?

I am sure there are many reasons why no leaders have appeared lately. Perhaps the media scrutinizes in such a way that it scares people from stepping forward. Maybe families hold future leaders down because of fear of repercussion or harm to the person or their loved ones. I don't know why we lack leaders today. I just know we need them.

What I Know | Dale Fushek

It's time to pray. It's time to encourage each other to have courage. It's time to be filled with hope. We need someone -- man or woman -- who can call us and lead us to someplace we have never been before: a place of goodness, faith, and dignity.

> A leader is not just an example of a particular virtue or good trait; leadership is a gift that goes far beyond being a role model.

Others

What I Know | Dale Fushek

I need – we all need – to stop expecting perfection from people we love.

Others

I know my expectations of others must change.

I have high expectations of myself. I always want to be a person who responds to life with integrity, love, and hard work. And, even though I don't want to beat myself up if I fall short, I never want to settle by giving an average amount of effort, or just being sort of truthful. I want to use every opportunity I have to learn how to love. I have and will always expect more of myself.

To be honest, I also want to have high expectations of others. Especially in a professional setting, I always want to assume that others will do quality work and make an effort to do what is right. As an employer, I have always tried to call my fellow workers to do their best and to be their best. I am sure these expectations have been hard on some, but for the most part, they have helped people to shine.

So, what is the issue? The issue comes with personal relationships. For people I am close to, I can often count on them to do things they almost can't or don't want to do. I can expect someone to put the same amount of energy into a friendship that I do. I can set expectations that someone else will love me with the same intensity that I love them. And, many times, I expect those close to me to know what I know. These types of expectations cause me to be hurt and disappointed when others fail to meet my standards.

Alcoholics Anonymous (AA) has a saying, "Expectations are premediated resentments."

What I Know | Dale Fushek

In other words, our expectations set us up to feel resentful, hurt, rejected, and unloved. We cause these ourselves.

I need -- we all need -- to stop expecting perfection from people we love. Our false expectations make it so that we don't accept or enjoy people as they are. God is our role model in doing this. God certainly calls us to be all we can be, but His love is unconditional. He accepts us as we are. We can do the same for each other.

Over the years, I have seen many children and teens be destroyed by their parents' expectations. I have also seen many marriages be harmed and many friendships broken. It simply is not worth it to demand others to meet our expectations in order to keep us happy.

On a personal note, I know that over the years I have held others to standards they couldn't meet. I need to keep growing and learning how to be more loving and accepting.

I will continue to hold high standards for myself. I will continue to hold high standards for my doctors and the professional people I deal with. I want to have high standards for those who work with me. But, I will lower my expectations for others with whom I share personal relationships.

Bruce Lee said, "I'm not in this world to live up to your expectations and you are not in this world to live up to mine."

When I first heard this, it sounded kind of negative. However, he is right.

P

Prayers

What I Know | Dale Fushek

I know prayer is not what I thought it was.

I have been praying for decades. In fact, I am a professional prayer person. And yet, I keep learning that prayer is not what I thought it was.

I thought prayer was all about words we say to God. Now, I understand that words have little to do with real prayer that comes from the heart.

So many different people have their own definitions of prayer. TV evangelist Joyce Meyer said, "Prayer is simply talking to God like a friend and should be the easiest thing we do each day."

Mahatma Gandhi said, "Prayer is a confession of one's own unworthiness."

The great spiritual writer Henri Nouwen said, "Prayer is not as much based on our desire for God. It is God's passionate pursuit of us that calls us to prayer."

And Mother Teresa said, "God speaks in the silence of the heart. Listening is the beginning of prayer."

I like the perspective that people like Henri Nouwen and Mother Teresa offer about prayer. For them, prayer is more about listening and being pursued by the Divine.

What I have learned in my prayer journey is that the rote words I learned as a child are just the very beginning of prayer. Now I understand that prayer is about being.

Prayers

When Paul tells us to "pray always" in his letter to the Thessalonians, he is telling us that prayer is deeper than saying certain words. Prayer is an awareness of God.

Prayer is living in a consciousness of God's love and God's presence.

I am aware, as a Christian, that the followers of Jesus asked Him how to pray. His response was the prayer that Christians have prayed for two thousand years, the Lord's Prayer, or Our Father. And, obviously these beautiful words inspire us, and we have repeated them since our childhood.

But I believe Jesus was telling us something much more profound. He was calling us to a relationship of trust with our Father in heaven. He wasn't asking us to say words. He was calling us to a lifestyle. The Our Father is a way to live life with a radical new understanding. It is living as brothers and sisters in the Lord, united in our total and complete trust of a good, good Father.

When I pray now, I am. I am in the presence of God. I am aware of God's unconditional love and goodness. I am available to God. I am letting God pursue me. I am worshipping God by heaping praise upon the Divine Lover. I am fully human and fully alive.

The things I learned about prayer as a child were good for that time in my life. But I know I need to keep maturing, to continue to grow in wisdom and experience. None

What I Know | Dale Fushek

of us can function in the world today by acting on what we learned as a child. We need to pursue deeper insight and understanding in order to grow.

I am so grateful for people like Mother Teresa and Henri Nouwen who have challenged me to enter the world of contemplation. I now understand I don't need to run to the temple to gaze at God. I can become the temple and go within my heart to experience His awesomeness.

> I thought prayer was all about words we say to God. Now, I understand that words have little to do with real prayer that comes from the heart.

Q

Questions

What I Know | Dale Fushek

I know that God is not threatened by our questions.

As I taught Bible study recently, a man interrupted the discussion and asked, "If God made everything, why did He make Satan?"

His question was a good one. I went on and gave the best answer I could about love needing free will. I explained that God could create all the robots He wanted, but if He wanted to be loved and to share His love, He needed to give some creatures the ability to choose not to love. At the end, I think the gentleman understood a bit more. And, even though I asked for a raise since I was doing "hazardous duty" work, I was grateful he felt free to ask the question.

Throughout my four decades in ministry, I have done a lot of work with teens. Kids have the ability to ask hard questions, and to push for authentic answers.

I say, "Good for them." And good for everyone, of any age, who asks sincere but difficult questions.

There was a time in the church that questions were frowned upon. Some people perceived questions as a rejection of authority or a rejection of faith. They are neither one.

God is not threatened by our ability to think or reason. He gave us those abilities. He wants us to use our minds to search for the truth. Science is not the enemy of religion.

Questions

Neither is reason. Our faith can be built by searching, seeking, asking, probing, and doing our best to go deeper into our understanding of God.

Elie Wiesel stated, "I questioned God's silence. I don't have an answer for that. Does it mean that I stopped having faith? No, I have faith, but I question it."

Elie was a Romanian-born American professor, writer, and Nobel Laureate who wrote about his experiences in concentration camps during the Holocaust. Who could doubt that Wiesel had reason to question God's silence?

Within the Bible itself, we see the psalmist questioning God. For instance, Psalm 10 states, "Why, O Lord, do you stand far away? Why do you hide yourself in times of trouble?"

If King David can question God, we can as well.

Questions about religion should always be asked in a sincere and respectful way. I am not suggesting a free for all. But at the same time, we need to know that God is not intimidated by our searching. God is not angered by our doubts. And, even if a religious leader is upset by a question, God honors the sincerity of our hearts.

As a pastor, I always want our community members to ask questions. I think it is good to ask questions not only about religion but about family, country, history, and morality. The deepest thinkers have only gotten to where they are by

What I Know | Dale Fushek

asking. The greatest theologians arrived at faith because they doubted.

The great spiritual writer C.S. Lewis was a convert from atheism. He shares in his writings that it was his late-night talks with friends like Henry Victor Dyson and J. R. R. Tolkien that allowed him to ask his questions and share his doubts that eventually brought him to faith. Lewis says, "I just passed on from believing in God to definitely believing in Christ-in Christianity. My long night talk with Dyson and Tolkien had a good deal to do with it."

In other words, we believers can do a great service to others by allowing them to share their questions and taking time to journey with them to the answers.

As believers, we want others to believe. But, like God, we cannot be afraid to face tough questions. God is not afraid of what others say. He is Who He is, and through searching, we may all come to know Him and His unconditional love.

R

Religion

What I Know | Dale Fushek

I know traditional religion just isn't working anymore.

I feel bad even saying these words. I have made a living and a life as part of traditional religion. Somehow, even saying it isn't working anymore seems to me, on a personal level, to admit defeat. But I have to be honest with myself and others.

Religion as many of us have known it isn't working in our world. That doesn't mean the world is "bad" or godless; it simply means that the world has changed.

There are many people who would disagree with me. I admit that Gallup polls indicate that the large majority of Americans are still believers. There are many megachurches that are still flourishing. And, similar to financial institutions during the banking crisis, there are churches that are simply too big to fail. But, when you move past the surface, the depth of the commitment of community members is not what it used to be.

Young people are exploring other alternatives as to how to conduct their spiritual lives. The truth is, when a lot of us old timers are gone, it is going to be a very different world.

One of the main reasons I believe traditional religion is becoming a dinosaur is that religion often has dealt with issues of suffering. Religion recalls the suffering of Jesus and constantly reminds us that we, too, must suffer. For many denominations, part of that suffering includes sitting through a worship service, mass, or long and irrelevant

Religion

preaching. Millennials are not buying it. They are changing our culture. Millennials are all about themselves, their comfort, their lives, their goals, their values, and their world.

They are not interested in keeping institutions on life support just for the sake of nostalgia. They regard many of our institutions as museums to be respected but that hold little relevance for them. Young people aren't striving to understand suffering and pain; they are trying to avoid or eliminate them.

Young people are seeking spirituality. Young celebrities are going to Hillsong Wednesday night services where they are mesmerized by great music, dynamic preaching, and a spirit of acceptance of each other. Spiritual Sundays are quickly becoming a thing of the past. Sunday now belongs to the NFL.

This new type of religious experience seems to be the wave of the future. When older Americans die off, our churches will become like churches in Europe that are either closed or run by government departments of museums and history. I might add that there are many middle-aged and older people who are on the same philosophical page as our young people.

Many spiritual writers are saying the same thing.

Author Mark Batterson states in his book *Primal* that Christianity has lost its soul and must seek to reform itself or die. He calls us not to look ahead but to look back at our roots

What I Know | Dale Fushek

and renew our spiritual lives by returning to the teachings of Christ. "When you descend the flight of stairs into the soul of Christianity and everything is stripped away but its primal essence, what you're left with is the Great Commandment." (page 169)

In other words, religion today needs to be based on loving God and each other, and moving away from bingo, theological debates, power plays by leading clergy, and the preservation of meaningless institutions.

I do not believe faith is dying. Whether millennials agree or not, people still need help dealing with suffering and death. And whether church leaders like it or not, people (young and old) want a spirituality that helps them cope with their daily lives. And, they want a spirituality that helps our crazy world seem saner.

If religion (as we know it) does not come up with some new ways to influence our world, people will simply find what they need somewhere else. They have already started that process.

S

Stuff

What I Know | Dale Fushek

I know I have too much stuff.

I like things to be clean. I don't like messy. And, I especially don't like clutter.

I am not a hoarder. I don't keep things for no reason and I am always willing to throw away or give away stuff. If someone tells me they like something I have hanging on a wall or sitting on a table, I very often will hand the item to the person and say "Take it; enjoy it."

As generous as that sounds, don't be fooled. I simply know that I have too many material possessions. There are times when I am out shopping (which I enjoy), and I want to buy something new. I think about it and I know in my heart I have nowhere to hang it or put it. So, giving something away creates an opening for something new.

I think many of us are "stuff-aholics." We collect things for a variety of reasons: (1) we think they will be valuable someday, or (2) we have items that have been given to us and we want to keep them for sentimental reasons; (3) we are fear based and we are afraid to give anything away, or (4) we simply lack the generosity to give to others. For many years, I kept a closet full of rugs and pillows just in case I ever needed an "emergency rug" to replace one I already had on the floor. In other words, sometimes we aren't even rational when it comes to collecting and keeping things.

Most of us are not called to a life of poverty. We are not St. Francis or Mother Teresa. We want to live in a nice house

Stuff

that is comfortable and beautiful. And, I believe that for most of us, that is what God wants for us as well.

I also believe, that God does not want us to be so caught up in our own comfort and our own possessions that we forget to give to others and to enrich the lives of other people. Many years ago, I saw a bumper sticker that read, "Live simply, so others may simply live." I think there is wisdom in that saying.

God is calling all of us to live more simply. Simplicity allows us the freedom to love, to give, to share, and to unburden ourselves from the burden of stuff.

A good way to know whether you have too much stuff is to close your eyes and imagine moving to a new location. If the task seems overwhelming, it's time to start unloading. I recently started going through closets and drawers and I realized that once again, I needed to make some changes. Then, I looked under my bed. I could open a gift store just from stuff I put there because I had no place else to store it.

Stuff is neither good nor bad. It is just stuff. If it enhances the quality of our lives, it is good. If we need to rent space in a storage facility just to hang onto stuff we will never use, it's time to sell, give, or throw it away.

I read a quote by someone named Susan Wright who observed, "Just because something belongs to you doesn't mean you should keep it for the rest of your life. Things are meant to be transitory."

What I Know | Dale Fushek

As I write this chapter, I feel like I am preaching. I guess I am. Just know I am preaching to myself.

I tell you, as I am telling myself, to enjoy the blessings God has given you. But, don't hang onto stuff too long.
Don't become selfish and lose the importance of generosity. Don't become so tied to your possessions that the very things that are meant to bring joy and comfort, now become a burden. And don't kick the can down the street so that at a later time your kids are stuck deciding what is valuable and what to keep.

I assure you, it will only make them feel guilty if you force those decisions on them. And they may end up holding onto stuff too long because they don't want to get rid of things that you may have valued, whether you actually did or not.

T

Types of People

What I Know | Dale Fushek

I know there are two types of people in this world.

I learned a long time ago there are two types of people in this world, As I say this, I am sure that some of you are thinking, "Good job. You noticed there are men and women!"

That's not what I was thinking! Clearly, there are many ways to divide people into separate categories: givers and takers, joiners and loners, fun and boring. I am not talking about any of these classifications, either. I am talking specifically about introverts and extroverts.

Introverts are generally regarded as the quiet folks who are not very out-going. Introverts are usually shy, reluctant to join in, unlikely to accept a social invitation.

Extroverts are generally defined as talkative, outspoken, often loud, and the opposite of shy. They tend not to be reluctant to speak or perform in front of others. On a deeper level, I have heard the opinion expressed that introverts are those who are drained emotionally and psychologically by being with others. And in contrast, extroverts are those who are recharged by being with other people.

These distinctions may be true. However, I would like to add two more distinctions to the list. And, I believe, these distinctions will help clarify why so many marriages, friendships, and work relationships run into trouble with communication between the people involved. Introverts think, then they talk. Extroverts talk, then they think. Let me explain.

Types of People

An introvert doesn't want to share their thoughts or feelings until they have time to process. So, when pressured by an extrovert, they want to withdraw from the conversation because they are not ready to talk. Quite often, the extrovert is offended by this withdrawal and doesn't understand why the introvert is walking away.

The extrovert may even feel rejected. In the mind of the introvert, however, they are just being honest because they haven't figured out yet what they are feeling.

An extrovert processes by talking out loud. It's only when they say something and hear it, that they know whether they meant what they just said. They might say several different things until they hit on one thought or feeling that expresses what is going on inside of them.

Let me give you an example. An introvert goes to the door, looks outside, stops, thinks, processes, and finally says, "I think I need a jacket today."

An extrovert goes to the same door, looks outside, and says, "I think I will wear a jacket. No, wait. I don't want to carry a jacket all day. It's supposed to rain. Maybe I need a rain coat. Never mind, no jacket. I will be indoors most of the day."

The extrovert becomes impatient waiting for an answer from the introvert. The introvert goes crazy pulling a jacket out of the closet for the extrovert, then putting it away. And, then bringing it out again.

What I Know | Dale Fushek

Why does any of this matter? When we understand we are not all alike, it becomes much easier to communicate and appreciate one another.

If two introverts marry, they are often the ones sitting quietly in a restaurant having dinner. If two extroverts marry, neither one listens and there may be chaos. Dinner will certainly be loud.

If introverts and extroverts understand and are patient with each other, they can have a rich relationship.

We don't all need to be alike to get along. We are each different and have unique personalities. But, when we are kind to each other and try to understand each other, we can create a better environment that allows us to be ourselves, to thrive, and to love each other.

U

United States

What I Know | Dale Fushek

I believe that our nation, our culture, is struggling with PTSD. I believe it stems back to 2001 and the events of 9-11 (September 11, 2001).

United States

I know our nation has many problems.

I tend to be patriotic. I love our nation and I am very loyal to the United States. I also know that our nation has many problems and we all need to pull together so we can deal with them.

Let me name just a few: lack of leadership, lack of unity, greed, an immoral media, inequity, violence, crime, and hate. It will require a lifetime of hard work for us to overcome these issues. And in addition to these issues, I believe there is one issue nobody is talking about.

Most people are familiar with the term "PTSD," which is the acronym for post-traumatic stress disorder. PTSD is usually defined as a mental condition that was caused by an event or series of events that result in an individual to responding to life events with inappropriate or severe physical or emotional reactions. Some of the events that can cause PTSD include war, violence, car crashes, domestic abuse, sexual assault, and natural disasters. PTSD can cause immense harm to an individual and to their family. It is usually necessary to undergo intensive therapy and sustain a strong emotional support system in order to manage this condition.

Many of us know individuals who served in the military who are struggling. Most of us have seen television programming that depict people who burdened by this terrible disorder. And most of us respond with great compassion when

What I Know | Dale Fushek

dealing with someone who is suffering.

I would like to submit my theory about what is happening in the USA. I believe that our nation, our culture, is struggling with PTSD. I believe it stems back to 2001 and the events of 9-11 (September 11, 2001). Our nation was attacked, and before our own eyes we saw the destruction of lives and property. I had a member of my church die in the collapse of the twin towers at the World Trade Center. To watch those buildings fall and know that he was there was traumatic. Trying to comfort his wife and two children was hard. And afterward, taking calls from officials in New York saying they had identified pieces of his bones was extremely emotional.

I realize that those born in the late 1990s and at the beginning of the new millennium do not remember these events firsthand and aren't as impacted. But the images from that day are seared into the minds and hearts of those of us who witnessed the violence and killing that took place that tragic day. In a sense, our innocence was lost, and it changed us. It changed our nation. I believe our culture has PTSD.

The symptoms of PTSD include flash backs, nightmares, depression, anxiety, withdrawal, avoidance, repression, emotional numbing, physical pain, hyper-arousal, fear of threats, irritability, and shame. Not everyone with PTSD experiences all these symptoms. If you consider how we are as a nation today, you will see that many of these

United States

symptoms manifest themselves in how we exist on a daily basis. I believe a lot of our anger, fear, irritability, hate and numbing could continue to plague us for a long time -- and if we don't deal with our underlying issues, we will never heal as a nation.

Because of our experiences associated with 9-11, many of us regard caravans of people coming to our borders from South America as an invasion of our nation. They raise fear inside of us and that those coming to the border want to harm us. Rational or not, we have to acknowledge these fears and admit that we have them so that we can cope with them.

Others among us have become numb and won't even acknowledge the possibility that terrorists may be coming through our borders illegally. It's not one party or one point of view that has become emotionally messed up -- it's all of us. And, we have seemed to have lost our ability to understand and listen to each other. This lack of understanding makes the symptoms of PTSD seem even more evident.

Therapists tell us there are treatments to help with PTSD. Treatments include a lot of listening, understanding, and ways to interrupt the negative thought patterns and associations of PTSD. I don't know what the answer is to dealing with these symptoms collectively as a society. But I do know we need to start healing, and that we need each other's understanding to heal.

What I Know | Dale Fushek

I want our nation to heal. I pray for unity, prosperity, security, and hope. But we must admit that we are continuing to hurt because of the traumatic events that happened at the World Trade Center. Let's start talking openly about what happened and how it has affected us. Maybe we can help each other find peace and wholeness.

V

Victory

What I Know | Dale Fushek

I know God defines victory differently than we do.

When I was a kid, I hurried to do homework and chores so I could watch my favorite television show. It was, I am embarrassed to say, *Roller Derby*. I loved the team called the Thunderbirds and I would actually cry when they lost. Please keep in mind that I was very young and had very little perspective on life. I am older now and allegedly wiser. I don't care about the Thunderbirds, anymore. However, I still want my teams to win and can get pretty upset when they don't. I can lose perspective from time to time.

We all want to win. It doesn't matter what the competition is. It feels better to experience the "thrill of victory" than the "agony of defeat" as the old tagline of The Wide, Wide World of Sports used to say. We Americans are especially opposed to losing. Our current president is big on winning. In fact, during the 2016 campaign he said, "If I'm president, we will win in everything we do."

Winning is fun. And, it is good in so many ways. It can be a great boost to self-esteem and self-image. Athletes work hard to improve their performance and get better and better so they can be victorious. The great football coach Vince Lombardi said, "Winning isn't everything; it's the only thing."

He pretty much summed up how most athletes and teams feel, and almost every fan who ever put on a team shirt and screamed in front of a television screen.

The question is, "How does God define victory?"

Victory

The answer is, He defines winning as us putting our trust in Him and giving up control. Victory usually means getting our own way and having our will overpower any resistance. Defeat usually means that someone else has control and their will is in charge.

Victory in Christ is letting go of control and accepting His will for us. God wills eternal life for us. He wills for us to die to sin, die to our ego, and die to putting our wishes above His will.

The Bible is clear in its teaching that we are to seek victory in Christ. St. Paul says, "But thanks to God, who gives us the victory through our Lord Jesus Christ. Therefore, my beloved brothers, be steadfast, immovable, always abounding in the work of the Lord, knowing that in the Lord your labor is not in vain." (1 Cor. 15:57-58)

The actor Charlie Sheen attempted to portray the ways of the world as trendy, or cool. Sheen said, "Only thing I am addicted to is winning. Every day is filled with just wins. All we do is put wins in the record book."

Of course, we soon discovered that Sheen was losing his job on television, losing any respect he had built in his professional life, and on the verge of losing his life from substance abuse. There was nothing cool about what "winning" was doing to his life.

We must be willing to see victory and winning through God's eyes. To surrender to God is to win. We can be vic-

What I Know | Dale Fushek

torious over all the earth by believing and following Jesus. In the end, He wins over all. And, He invites us to share in His victory.

Victory in Christ is letting go of control and accepting His will for us.

W

Wonder

What I Know | Dale Fushek

I know we have lost our sense of wonder.

My favorite book is called *Dangerous Wonder: The Adventure of Childlike Faith*. It was written by my friend, Michael Yaconelli. Michael died in a car accident in 2003. In the book, Michael states, "Dullness is more than a religious issue, it is a cultural issue. Our entire culture has become dull. Dullness is the absence of the light in our souls. Look around. We have lost the sparkle in our eyes, the passion in our marriages, the meaning in our work, the joy in our faith."

In other words, we have lost our sense of wonder and amazement. The word "wonder" comes from the Old English term wunder, which meant a marvel or a marvelous thing. Because we have become numb or dull in our souls, we have lost our true ability to marvel. In the course of a day, there are many "wonder-filled" things placed in our lives by God. Some days, it is a sunset, a mountain view, a person, or a lesson. And so often, we don't notice it or respond to it.

I remember several years ago I had my first echocardiogram. I do not know if the technician knew who I was, but she certainly knew who she was. She was a deeply spiritual person. As she performed the test, she talked about the blood flow in my heart. She kept referring to how incredible God was to have put the human person together the way He had. She told me to look at a chamber and see how God brought blood from here into this chamber

Wonder

and then sent it into this chamber. As I watched, I started to cry. The medical test I was there to take seemed to fade into the background as I had a spiritual experience.

Recently I was led our community in a Bible study about the book of Job. My favorite part of Job is the dialogue between him and God. God describes how magnificent His power is and questions Job as to why he would doubt Him. Job responds by saying (Job 40:3-5), "I am speechless, in awe -- words fail me. I should never have opened my mouth. I've talked too much. I'm ready to shut up and listen."

We should become more like Job. It's time for us to shut up and listen. And, it is time for us to open our eyes to the wonder of God, creation, goodness, and love.

Children seem to have a natural sense of wonder. Unfortunately, video games and digital screens are killing it. We as a culture are standing by and watching wonder wither. We need to encourage it in our young ones. And, we need to wake up our old souls and allow ourselves to be in awe of all that God has done.

Yaconelli went on to say, "Immorality is much more than adultery and dishonesty; it is living drab, colorless, dreary, stale, unimaginative lives. The greatest enemy of Christianity may be people who say they believe in Jesus Christ but are no longer astonished and amazed."

Our souls and our hearts need to wake up. The wonder

What I Know | Dale Fushek

of creation is amazing, but it is nothing compared to the wonder of God's unconditional love. Our prayer lives and our daily lives will be much richer if we gift ourselves with WONDER, MARVEL, and AWE.

It's time for us to shut up and listen. And, it is time for us to open our eyes to the wonder of God, creation, goodness, and love.

X

X-ray

What I Know | Dale Fushek

I know we believe we can see into another person's heart.

The X-ray machine changed medicine. I didn't realize X-ray technology dated back to 1895 and Wilhelm Rontgen who discovered that a person's interior structures could be seen with the help of photography. In fact, just a year later, X-ray was used for the first time in surgery. Today, through MRIs and digital X-rays, doctors can observe a patient's organs and blood flow as never before.

Even though X-ray is so commonly used today, it has never been able to see inside a person's intentions. A machine can detect medical issues in the physical human heart, but it cannot reveal emotions, feelings, or motives – our "heart of hearts."

We often think we know what is behind someone else's thoughts and behaviors. However, we actually can truly only guess what someone else is feeling. And when we do guess, all we can do is form a judgment about someone's intentions. We can't know for certain what a person is thinking unless they choose to tell us.

There are no machines that reveal the emotions of the human heart. That is why only the individual and God know what someone is thinking.

Jesus was very clear in His teaching that we should not judge. I used to say flippantly, "Jesus told us we could not judge, but He didn't say we couldn't have an opinion."

X-ray

I was wrong. We can certainly have an opinion about someone's behavior, but we can never know what God sees. In the Gospel of Matthew (7:1-2), Jesus says, "Do not judge, or you too will be judged. For the same way you judge others, you will be judged, and with the measure you use, it will be measured to you."

In other words, let God judge. We should avoid trying to take His place. He's got this task covered and doesn't need our help.

However, it is important to remember that when we refuse to judge, others may believe we are condoning someone's bad behavior. This isn't the truth, but there will be those who insist that it is. It doesn't matter.

When we refuse to condemn someone, it does not mean we accept unacceptable behavior. We can determine from our own moral standards when someone's behavior is troubling. We simply don't know their motivation or what is in their heart. And we are not called to be their judge. We are told to love them anyway.

The first commandment tells us, "I am the Lord your God, you shall have no false gods before me."

When we judge, we break this commandment. We are taking the place of God. And most likely, that sin is worse than the sin we are judging.

We cannot know the heart of another. So, we need to stay

What I Know | Dale Fushek

in our own heart and make sure we are acting as Christ called us to act. We don't have X-ray vision. Let's let doctors use X-ray machines for physical healing, and let God use His own method to see inside the hearts of our brothers and sisters.

There are no machines that reveal the emotions of the human heart.

Y

Yesterday

What I Know | Dale Fushek

I know we must come to grips with our past.

We are frequently told not to dwell on the past. That is certainly excellent advice. We don't need to re-live the past, or focus on regrets or past mistakes. But e can't ignore the past, either.

The past is part of who we are. It got us to where we are today, in one way or the other. And when we work to understand the choices we have made and the experiences we have had, it makes our future better and brighter.

The philosopher Socrates stated, "The unexamined life is not worth living." He made this statement at his trial for corrupting youth. He was given the death sentence, yet what he said is still true today.

We need to examine our lives and our choices so we can heal, grow, and become better people. We must look at our past with an open mind so we know who we are, and why. Soren Kierkegaard, also a philosopher, had a similar outlook as Socrates. Kierkegaard said, "Life can only be understood backwards; but it must be lived going forward."

I try to reflect each night on the day I just lived. I try to understand where I encountered God and where I missed God. I reflect on the recent past to see how I could have lived a more loving life. I try to look back at the good and bad experiences of my life to understand mistakes I have made. I know I have been forgiven for these mistakes, but if I can understand them, I can avoid making them again in the future.

Yesterday

We all have things in our past that we would prefer weren't pictured on a billboard along a busy highway. There are times we have hurt those around us, and times when we have been deeply hurt by those we love. We have been through divorces and break-ups of relationships and friendships. If we can honestly understand a divorce, we can prevent it in a new relationship.

We have lost jobs, financial mistakes, moral failures, human frailty, and broken hearts to examine at night when we are alone with our thoughts. We have had times we were distant from God. What caused us to go and grow away from God? By facing these issues and dealing with them, we stand a better chance at creating a better future, one day at a time.

Part of coming to grips with our past is accepting the mercy and forgiveness of God. God is a radical forgiver. No matter what we have done, His mercy is bigger than any of our sins. We can also use our reflection to muster up a sense of self-forgiveness. If God can let go, so can we.

There is a story about St. Augustine that touches me. He was quite the serial sinner. After his conversion, he became a priest and a bishop. Some of his parishioners asked him how he felt about being bishop of a city where he committed so much debauchery. Augustine responded by asking them if they were speaking of his sinfulness. He went on to say, "Oh, you mean my sins? My sins are my friends because they are the ones who taught me about the mercy of God."

What I Know | Dale Fushek

Augustine came to grips with his past and saw it through the eyes of God. It's a great example for all of us. May we face our pasts with honesty and with the love of God.

Mother Teresa of Calcutta left us with some words to live by when she said, "Yesterday is gone. Tomorrow has not yet come. We have only today. Let us begin."

> Part of coming to grips with our past is accepting the mercy and forgiveness of God.

Z

Zorro

What I Know | Dale Fushek

Zorro is Spanish word for "fox." The person Zorro -- who for a number of years was portrayed in glorious black and white on a popular television show and adored by a generation of kids -- was a fictional character who supposedly lived in the late 1700s.

Zorro was a vigilante in the style of Robin Hood who defended common people against corrupt officials and villains. He wore a black cape, hat, and mask and carried a long, sharp sword. Whenever he defeated an opponent or won a battle, he slashed a large "Z" in three quick strokes on a nearby object to mark that Zorro had been there and was the victor.

Unfortunately, you and I don't have swords. We don't make a physical sign to show where we have been. But the truth is, you and I want to leave our mark on the world by making it a better place.

Ralph Waldo Emerson said, "To leave the world a bit better, whether by a healthy child, a garden patch or a redeemed social condition; to know that even one life has breathed easier because you have lived -- that is to have succeeded."

Many people – famous and not famous -- have remarks similar to Emerson. Country singer Carrie Underwood said, "Successful people have a responsibility to make the world a better place and not just take from it."

My friend Kevin Johnson, the former NBA star said, "I

would like to somehow make the community I live in a better place to live."

Like Kevin, I want to make a difference. I want the world to be a better place because of me. I hope some of the things I have been involved in -- Life Teen, Paz De Cristo, St. Tim's Academy, Mother Teresa's House in Phoenix (Gift of Mary), The Praise and Worship Center -- will be a blessing to the world. I pray that long after I am gone these organizations will continue to minister to God's people, and to people who are still looking for Him.

I also pray that the love I have shared with others will make a lasting difference in the world. Perhaps the love I allowed to flow through me will continue to flow through others for a long time.

No matter how old we are, it is good for all of us to reflect on our legacy. The word "legacy" means to transmit something from one generation to the next. A legacy can be money, personal property, a building or house, or a lesson. Our legacy can be an example of a life fully lived.

The marks that Zorro left have disappeared. Young people don't know who Zorro was and the television show has been off the air for years. The huge Zs that appeared on the walls after he defeated his criminal enemies are gone. In fact, the marks on walls that kids left playing Zorro are also plastered and painted over.

But, through Christ, we can leave a legacy that won't go

What I Know | Dale Fushek

away. Scripture tells us that love never dies (I Corinthians 13:8). Our legacy of love and loving acts can live on for years after we are gone. Our mark may not be as flashy as Zorro's, but it certainly can be more enduring.

Our legacy can be an example of a life fully lived.

Conclusion

Conclusion | Jody Serey

My least favorite expression used to be, "It was a learning experience."

My husband, David – who is much more philosophical about executing the occasional spectacular belly-flop off the high dive of life – is known for saying those five words. I am known for sometimes glaring at him when he does.

But the simple fact is that if you are lucky enough to survive the idiocy of your youth, the wear and tear of your 30s and 40s, and the accumulated challenges of middle age and your golden years – you do learn things. Experiences collect in your history like barnacles on the underside of an old ship, or like pearls in oysters – depending on what events and circumstances have transpired and how you regard them.

"It was a learning experience."

David has applied that perspective to failed recipes, failed business ventures, failed hopes, failed dreams, and failed relationships. I have told him more than once that I wish I could fully embrace that phrase and make it a mantra. He said he isn't going to hold his breath.

When Fr. Dale said that he wanted to summarize some of the nuggets of his learned experiences in a book, I knew immediately that fate had brought me back around to face my five-word nemesis. I just hoped Fr. Dale wouldn't look back on this venture and say, "It was a learning experience."

Conclusion

Yet, it was, and not in the ways I might have anticipated.

What I learned about Fr. Dale — whose friendship with David and me spans more than 40 years — is that he still has much to reveal. Because we have talked candidly for decades, I did have an inkling of what he knows, what he believes. But as he observes, only God knows what is in a person's heart.

I have often told Fr. Dale that I view friendship as a sacred bond, and as the very foundation for all other relationships, human and divine. Jesus' own words as recorded in John 15 were, "I have called you friends."

And yes, friendship continues to be a "learning experience," to quote my favorite philosopher, David Serey. But it is also the greatest treasure found on this earth, I believe.

This book is a gift from Fr. Dale to his friends, the ones he loves. I hope you discovered in it the small truths that led you to a deeper understanding of who he truly is.

Jody Serey
Spring 2019